CW00420563

20 – 80 Ti Management:

Time management from the inside out

Richard Ingate

Dedication

With gratitude to the coaches who expected me to step up to life and who have taught me so much, in particular Steve Chandler, Michael Neil and Steve Hardison, and to my parents who gave me a life to step up to.

Preface:

You have exactly as much time in your day as the most famous and successful person you admire. The may be many other differences between you, but this is the same. What you choose to create with your time is the next interesting question, and I chose the verb, 'create' very deliberately.

20/80 Time Management: Time Management From The Inside Out

Hello, and thank you for purchasing this ebook. You may also have received the audio version so you can work with any combination of reading and listening that works best for you. If you have any questions, you can contact me through my website, www.richardingate.com, I will be happy to hear from you.

You may think you have a problem with time management. Maybe you are running or trying to set up your own business and just don't have enough hours in the day. Perhaps you are working as a healer or therapist but feel burnt out and stressed yourself. You might be a heart / spirit centered practitioner who feels that life is a struggle to make enough money and to have enough time?

You are in the right place. This book will show you how to:

- save time
- make more money
- enjoy better quality of life

- understand the connection between self-care and productivity
- end procrastination

Who am I?

I am a Coach, NLP Master Practitioner, Hypnotherapist, Tai Chi enthusiast, long term meditator, and teach at a UK university joint venture. I struggled with balancing working for someone else with having a family, wanting to exercise, meditate and follow my spiritual practice, play music and build a business. What is in this book is what I wished I knew twenty years ago! It is knowledge that has been hard won from experience, making mistakes and trying things out. It is my sincere wish for you that you benefit from this information now, rather than having to wait like I did.

The rationale

The Pareto Principle is well known. 20% of what you do gets you 80% of your results. It follows that time management should be a small investment of your time and energy that rewards you with large and measurable results. It should not be tyranny by list! Neither should it take a long time to learn and begin to implement, which is why this is an ebook and not a weighty tome. By the way, yes, I do know it's called the

80/20 principle... I turned it round to emphasise the 20% that you actually do that has such a big effect.

Key understandings

These are the key principles to having a good relationship with time. If you get these right, you will evolve your own time management system that will be perfect for you.

Key understanding number 1 It's a myth, you know... You can't manage time.

Time is itself and some claim it is an illusion. Whatever it may or may not be, we cannot do anything to have more of it, or to recover it when it has gone. In the past, experts have used this fact to argue for having rigid priority systems and living your life by a painstakingly graded 'to do' list. This can work; it really can, especially in the short term if you have a particular project in mind, for example.

However, it really does not work as a long term solution and is a case of the tail wagging the dog. Many people start to work a priority system, such as the one featured in Brian Tracy's books. They start with good intentions, you may be one of them, I know I was. The system works for a little while, or at least until the first phone call or nasty email, or sick child takes you off track. Therein lies the problem, you start to live according to a list rather than being responsive to reality. Having said that, from a balanced foundation, priority systems do have a place and I will show you a priority system that you can use when you need to, later in this book.

The value of a priority system comes from the state of mind from which you use it.

If you implement a to do list and grading system from stress and anxiety, and a frantic feeling that you have to get everything done, then you may be more productive in the short term, but you will end up even more stressed than ever; and if you are a self employed practitioner, that is going to hurt your bottom line before long.

You can't manage time! What you will learn to be aware of and 'manage' is your state of mind and your own sense of balance and center. When these are in alignment, and when you make their alignment your focus, you will have all the time you need to do everything that you decide to do. You will still prioritise, but you will prioritise from a place of creativity and wisdom. I hope this strikes a chord for you. If it doesn't, bear with me and keep reading. If you put the ideas and the suggestions I give you here, into practice; you will experience the truth and the value for yourself.

Key understanding number 2: Busy is about your thoughts, not about your tasks

What does 'busy' mean to you?

For some it is exhilarating, for others it is something to sigh about. In either case, being busy is not about the number of tasks, it is about the perception we have of those tasks. If you don't want to do them (perhaps they are boring, or even someone else's 'busy work' that you have to endure) your mood will be low and you will easily go into overwhelm. From that low mood it is easy to slide into thoughts of giving up for the day, or becoming resentful, going for a cigarette, a drink or a doughnut! Your thoughts create your feelings and your feelings create your moods. Your moods lead to behaviour and negative moods are certainly not a good place to be in when you have to work with clients and want to creatively develop your business to new heights.

None of these feelings is actually a result of the workload; they are a result of our thoughts. A great instant antidote to 'overwhelm' from feeling that you are too busy is to use the 'post it' technique given later in this ebook.

'Busy' means you have more to do than you want to do at the moment of perception. The idea of having more to do than you want, is a thought. You only ever do one thing at a time. Read this again: you are only ever doing one thing at a time. Even if you think you are multi tasking (which usually means doing a few things badly), you are switching between tasks that you are doing bits of, one at a time.

A word about multi tasking. If you enjoy reading and watching television and doing the ironing at the same time, then do it for entertainment. As a means of productivity, multi tasking only detracts from focus and awareness. For a heart centered practitioner, working with awareness is part of our journey, so please don't get caught up in the mistake of multi tasking. This is especially true when you are working with clients. **Being present is the main time management technique you need when you are working with a client.**

Key understanding number 3: Effective time management centers on self-care first and then appropriate response to tasks second.

This doesn't seem relevant at first sight, does it? How can self-care have anything to do with time management? You might even be thinking, I haven't got enough time for self-care any way!

Time management has nothing to do with managing time. Time cannot be managed, you can only organise yourself. How you do that is dependent on your state of well-being. If you are in a good state of mind, and, like a roly poly doll you naturally return to a state of well-being, then organising and prioritising are not problems. You know what to do and you get on with it, without any strain. If you are not in a good state of well-being, if you are stressed, tired and feeling negative, you are going to make poor decisions about how to manage your day. You will trip over stumbling blocks that are just not there when you are in a good state. You do not need a technique to overcome the stumbling blocks, you need to get back to a good state of mind...because then the blocks vanish...

I remember one of my mentors being asked a question about what would he do if Warren Buffet or Bill Gates lost their memory and in that state came to see him as a coach and ask for advice on how to start a business. What would he do? Would he help them start up a business and teach them some techniques, or would the coachl **help them to remember who they were?**

A state of well-being from which your creativity and action flows, is your natural state. The real work is to remember...

That is why you need a robust self-care practice and that needs to become your priority. Your well-being is the crop and your self-care is the fence around the crop. Start thinking about what you do for your own self-care.

Key understanding number 4: Priority systems are a useful tool and a terrible master

If you have no clue about organising your time, priority systems are a useful place to start. These are basically making a list of what you have to do and labelling each task as an A, B or C according to how urgent and important they are. Then you start doing the urgent and important ones first. They can be a valuable tool as long as you use them and not the other way round! I will outline the priority system I recommend later in this book. Planning your day is a good habit to get in to, and a good place to start working with the technique side of time management. It doesn't need to be difficult, just sit down and think about what is important to you to do today, write it down and make a start. No fuss, no strain...

Key understanding number 5: The best time management system for you is individual to you.

If only because one size really does not fit all. You have to find out what combination of ingredients works for you. This may change according to what you have going on. As I write this, I only have a few non business items on a single post it list. That is because I know that all my focus is on writing this so I just need to track a few other jobs that I don't want to get missed. I certainly don't need to write down every single job I might get round to...because I won't. That would just be more thoughts chasing round the hamster wheel.

The 'how to' part: From fire fighting to direction
If you are:
- in overwhelm
- if you feel stressed out and anxious about your business

- and you are not doing the things that are important to you and nurture you
- if you have so much other stuff to do

You are fire fighting, and not moving with purpose and direction. The very first thing you need to do is to decide what you want your wonderful life to be like. What do you want your career to be like, your spiritual life, your health and fitness, your relationships, and any other area that makes sense to you. This is what Steven Covey calls 'beginning with the end in mind'.

What do you want? Use the worksheet that accompanies this book or just make notes for yourself. Write a paragraph describing your ideal life.

Make sure you do this step. If you work the steps the steps will work for you. If you don't, well it's nice to have known you. To be blunt, if you don't take action you will still be complaining about the same problems the same time next week/month/year...

Remember to make what you write your ideal life in the sense of your best balance for doing the work you love and living the healthy engaged and fulfilling life that is your potential, rather than a lottery win fantasy!

Do remember to make it a life that you would actually want, not a life you think you 'should' want to want...

Where are you now?

For the same areas as in the last exercise, where are you now?

Make sure you cover the same areas as you did in your ideal life. I am sure you can appreciate that what we are doing here is assessing what is important to you and where you are now in relation to your values for your life.

This is actually a foundation for time management. It is a preparatory step. Until you know what your values are and what direction you want to go in, time management is actually meaningless. You could overlay a priority system on to your life as it is now, and it could absolutely make your situation worse. Sometimes we misuse time management as a whip to make ourselves do more work, when what we actually needed for our well-being was to take a walk...

And that is also true the other way round, although it may not be as obvious. I want you to discover your values, the goals that those values naturally express as, and your current balance in relation to those goals and values. This doesn't always mean letting yourself off the hook, anymore than it always means 'going that extra mile'.

For example, you may be in a low mood but it is on your schedule to go to the gym. Well, once you realise that 'not wanting to go to the gym is thought, rather than a problem 'out there', then into the gym you go, and do what you can with patience and intention!

This is definitely not about being lazy. It is about creating conditions for your state of mind to be able to elevate, to rise up, by understanding that what we experience is our own thought.

What we experience is our own thought.

Here are the exercises for this part again, (just in case a few of you did not do them the first time...

Areas of life: examples for you to adjust as you see fit.

finance

career

relationships

health

spiritual

self-care

For each area do the following:

example: career (ideal)

I have an annual income of £ (fill in your own number!) which I receive from my coaching programmes and products. I spend a maximum of two hours a day face to face with clients over skype or in person and another two hours a day developing products and courses and writing (all of which I really enjoy) I love the lifestyle which this combination of passive and active income allow me to have and spend 6 months of the year living abroad, using the internet to continue my business where ever I am.

career (current)

I have an annual income of £ (fill in your own numbers which I receive from teaching part time and coaching. I am developing my first products and working with coaches myself, to build my business. I am overwhelmed with the amount of things I need to do, in what is effectively two jobs.

As I mentioned above, you can go through this exercise in a notebook or use the sheets that should come with this book.

Here is a really cool technique you can use straight away to help you transition from fire fighting to direction: It's two really simple questions.

1. When you look at your ideal life, **what is one thing that if you started it or did more of it would take you in the right direction and support your well-being?**

answer_____

_____

_____

2. What is one thing that **if you stopped doing it or did less of it would help you go in your chosen direction and support your well-being?**

answer

_____

_____

Now use the extra time from stopping the negative one to start doing the positive one. No extra time required and you have let go of something holding you back and taken a positive step towards your well-being.

So, you have created a statement, a vision of your ideal life, an audit of your current life and identified one thing about the current situation to let go of, and one thing that will advance you in your chosen direction. You have begun to **move from fire fighting to purpose.**

What do you think would happen if you did the same exercise every week? What if you stopped doing one thing you don't like, or that doesn't support you, and started doing one thing you do like and that does support you?

Do you think that this process would contribute to your sense of well-being, as well as to your productivity?

How do you want to get there? / What shape supports your well-being?

Well-being is your natural state and is shown by predominantly good states of mind, with speedy lifting of negative states of mind, as well as naturally high levels of productivity. This isn't off topic. This is the heart of time management. If you are in a state of well-being, then knowing what to do and doing it are natural expressions of your unforced positivity. You may have experienced times when a certain task made you angry and frustrated, even depressed you. Then the next day, perhaps because you had read something uplifting, your inner state was elevated and the same task seemed inconsequential.

What I am saying here is that focusing on your well-being is what allows you to make the journey from where you are now to where you want to be... and *want* to make that journey. In your natural wellness you take inspired action on your goals and you make more money as an inevitable consequence. You are fluid and deal with what comes your way without being overwhelmed.

As a heart centered practitioner, your effectiveness with your clients is far more than a mechanical application of technique.

It's the interrelationship of your technique, your being and your client. If you are 'out of sorts' you have disconnected from the energy that makes you a great therapist, a great healer or coach. You have to get off the hamster wheel of thought...it's thought not reality. As you learn to do this, your balance gets better and you can move in response to life's events without strain.

Now that is heart centered time management!

Objection:

That all sounds wonderful for you but.... I have got small kids, a huge mortgage, noisy neighbours, a wife/husband who demands all my free time, a business that is struggling to make enough. I just don't have any time to manage...and my cat just died.

Answer:

The first step is about how you want things to be. Well-being is our natural state and our current mess is symptomatic of being out of tune with our own well-being. As soon as we allow, or create the conditions for our natural healthy state of mind to emerge, our time management 'problems' are more manageable.

From direction, to, packing for the journey

You have established a destination and seen where you are now in relation to that. You have seen that the central concept, an understanding of which will end overwhelm really quickly, is to **put your own well-being first**.

Put your own mask on first! If you have ever been on an aeroplane you will have heard this one, and it makes sense does it not? Put your own mask on first, or you will be no good to anyone. If you don't put your own mask on first you will struggle to organise your day and your clients will pick up that something isn't quite right with your energy.

Here is a metaphor. Tai Chi Chuan is a Chinese martial art. You may have seen movies of 'old' people moving really slowly...poor old things, too far gone to do real exercise! I used to live in Malaysia which has a large Chinese population. Tai Chi Chuan is very strong there. It can certainly be used for gentle exercise, but was brought over to Malaysia by dialect groups who were in physical conflict with other clans. It was brought over as a fighting art (and has remained such in Malaysia).

Why on earth am I telling you all this? To set up my point. A Tai Chi master will spend a significant amount of time training alone. He or she is doing those really slow movements so he/she can **work carefully with awareness** to bring every small part into balance and alignment. It is called '**connecting the structure**'.

It is only when the mind - body structure is in alignment, or in Tai Chi speak, 'central equilibrium' that the practitioner can usefully work with others and move appropriately and fluidly to deal with external force. Until then, the practitioner's body is holding too much tension to be able to move well and in holding too much tension the practitioner is insensitive to the application of external force until it becomes extreme...ie overwhelming.

Do you get the idea? If you do not take care of yourself, then you are so 'revved up' that you do not perceive something as needing a response until it is too far advanced.

That is part of how people become overwhelmed. When you do eventually notice, then it's like a snowball that has hurtled too near your face for you to move out of the way in time. Whereas, if you had been aware of it being thrown from a distance, you could have avoided it easily. To compound the situation, the shock of the snowball hitting you revs up your thoughts, and you become even more overwhelmed and less able to deal well with the next things that come along. So then you start trying to impose a time management system...

Of course it isn't going to work.

Focus on your self-care first. Put your own mask on first. As you come into your own 'central equilibrium' you will become more responsive AND more able to deal with what forces come your way. The less tension you are holding means the more strength you have available to use. It is by coming in to your balance that you can undertake the journey to your goals. It is in taking care of yourself first that you will save time and serve your clients better than ever before.

So, when you wake up at 3.00am in the morning anxious and overwhelmed by your life, realise that is a signal to 'take your foot off the gas pedal' and put your own mask on first. It is a signal to do something to take care of yourself. It is not a signal to try and solve the problem that woke you up! If you try to do that from a distressed state of mind, you will not make good decisions and probably end up with an even bigger mess to clear up. Negative feelings and distress are a signal to put your own mask on first and allow the thoughts to settle and then naturally rise.

Taking care of yourself is not the same as numbing yourself. Numbing yourself is actually another form of holding unnecessary tension. For example if I start to use alcohol to 'relieve' my stress I am actually putting myself in quite an extreme, chemically induced state. That always has less than useful consequences. Who wants to go to an alcoholic therapist? As a client you can pick up on the energy that your therapist is giving off, and you know when something is 'off'.

As a self employed therapist, the energy, the state of consciousness that you are coming from is the key ingredient. It is **that** that attracts your ideal clients. It is the marketing, the conversations you have with people, the articles you write, even the Facebook posts you make, **from your elevated state of mind** that resonates with your **ideal clients**.

Can you see how self-care is not an additional burden on your time, but actually the foundation of both your life and your business? If you do not take care of yourself, how can you be authentic about helping others?

If you are interested in exploring the notion of marketing from the heart, to your ideal client, go and have a look at www.sheelamasand.com. She is the coach who helped me to launch my business and so helped me to find you! I completely recommend her work.

Let me repeat the main point here. Self-care isn't something extra that you have to fit in to a day that is already too much to cope with. Self-care is the vital (in more than one sense) foundation from which your day unfolds.

When you pay attention / give yourself permission, to focus on your well-being, your outlook, your energy, your positivity are naturally elevated and you make better decisions.
Please read that part again: When your outlook, your energy, your positivity are naturally elevated **you make better decisions**.

When you make better decisions, you 'navigate by joy' (to borrow Michael Neil's expression), and you can then use time management tools with wisdom and in a way that supports both your business and your heart.

Do I need to labour this point? When we are stressed, tired, frightened, anxious, angry (and all of that stuff that comes to us all simply because we are human), we get lost in our thoughts and feelings. Our thoughts and feelings get all revved up, like getting stuck in mud in your car, and being so angry that you push down the accelerator pedal and spin your wheels so that you get more stuck. The thoughts and feelings are so strong that they totally convince us that they are real and that the world is actually like this.

We lose our equanimity, our 'unflappability', our balance. And then we make an important decision. Then we have a conversation with a potential client. Then we hit off an angry reply to a customer's email complaint.

And then, as I am sure you have realised, bad things happen! What happens next is that along with everything else that we have to deal with (that hasn't gone away in the meantime) we now have a mess that we have to clear up. Perhaps it's too late and we lose the client, or lose our relationship even. No small wonder that we are overwhelmed, especially as self employed people, often working on our own, because the bottom line is that we make money or we have nothing.

Now that is **a scary thought**, and that is the point. It's a scary...thought. The thought hooks into a feeling and the feeling is taken on as being about the world, rather than being a feeling. Then we act on the feeling as if it is about the world rather than recognising the feeling as being a feeling.

This realisation and the nurturing of this realisation is the starting place for joined up self-care. The going for a walk, learning meditation, or whatever you choose to do, then makes sense to you, rather than being an add-on that you have to fit in to the day.

It is not that meditation (for example) is going to make you a serene and blissed out 'super-therapist' wafting through your day to fame and fortune. The meditation gives you a context for understanding thought as thought, and so letting go. A good walk can have a similar result and **allow those creative insights through that will become your best decisions.**

It's not about technique. Technique is useful but technique will be bound by, limited by, whatever thoughts and state of mind we happen to be in. A great athlete, for example, has peerless technique but when they have an 'off day' their technique does not support them to play at the same level.

The technique of no technique

By this point I hope you understand that time management is an inside job, an inner game. **The most important element of time management is to value our feelings as clear information about whether our thinking is supporting us, or has led us astray.**

Thus designing a life and an attitude to life that nurtures your awareness of thought, as thought, rather than 'you' or 'the world' is time management at the highest level. When we use our awareness to allow our states of mind to rise up, we naturally become more productive and save time.

I have spent a long time explaining why time management is not effective just on the level of tips and techniques. So now I *am* going to offer some tips and techniques in the hope that you will **use them in the context of awareness**, and as a means of nurturing your well-being, rather than making yourself busier. That does not mean, by the way, if you are looking after your well-being that it is 'wrong' to organise an extra client session into your day. It is about the state of mind that you organise your day from.

Here are my two favourite priority systems. The first comes in the form of a story that I learned from Michael Neil. The story goes that one day a professor took a glass jar, some rocks, smaller stones, sand and water into the class. The professor asked the students how to get all of the items into the jar. After various combinations did not work the answer came that you have to put the big rocks in first, then the small stones, then the sand finds spaces around the small stones and lastly the water finds all the remaining free space.

It's the same with time management. You put the big rocks in first. What are the most important and obvious things that you need to do in a day? Of course this depends on what your goals are, doesn't it? I have daily routine big rocks, e.g. meditate, exercise and goal big rocks, such as writing this ebook, at the moment.

So I know I am going to work on these areas every day. I just put them into my routine at a specific time every day and get on with them. Anything else gets fitted around these big rocks in descending order of importance. If I have a lot on at a given time, I will use a list system, if not, I just do what occurs to me to do next.

Once you have taken care of the big rocks by putting them into a daily schedule, you can use the other one of my favourite systems. Make a list of whatever you think you should be doing and put one task on one post it note. Roughly stack the post its on top of each other in an order of importance of task, but don't spend too much thought on this step. Then take the first post it and get on with it as if it's the only thing on your mind to do. When you have finished, throw it away and start on the next one. Keep doing this in between your big rock tasks. **Make sure you have planned your day** to include self-care time.

If you are really chasing a lot of tasks and haven't yet come into a less busy balance, a good system to use for short periods of time is Mark Forster's list system. The basic idea is that you take a page of your notebook and rule a line down the middle. On the left side you write down absolutely every task you can think of that you need to do. Just use the left side and if you run out of space, go onto the next page, rule a line down the centre and continue.

When you have done that, read through your list and ask yourself what absolutely has to be done today, with no excuses and without fail. Transfer these items to the right hand column. These are your priority items. Start and carry on until you have done them. Do not do any task on the left of the page until the items on the right are done. One feature of this system is that once a list is done, it's closed. However many items you have on the right, cross out the rest of the page to 'close' it. Anything new goes on the next page and you won't look at it until you have completed the right hand column items of the first page.

If you are in a place where you need to take a lot of action for a while, then this is a great system to clear a lot of jobs in a short time. Such systems should be used sparingly. Your priority is to build a schedule that supports your well-being and well as your wealth and health, not to be a blazing star of activity that burns itself out.

What to do now

You have seen that the best use of time management is to support your well balanced life because the better mental and spiritual state you are in, the better decisions you will make, and the more value you will share with your clients.

I have encouraged you to focus on self-care as a way of elevating your state of mind, rather than trying to *frantically* save time and do more. You will save time and do more when you bring your life into the balance that is right for you.

On the foundation of all this I have offered you three techniques to organise the most important parts of your day, deal effectively with the rest, as well as an emergency system for short bursts of activity.

The next step I would suggest is that you build one particular activity into your day. **That is to begin your day with sitting comfortably with the beverage of your choice and creating / planning your day.** What is it that you *want to* do today? What do you really *want to* make your day about today?

Now that doesn't mean that you always can. Maybe not at first, but the more you navigate your life by 'joy', the more you will find that you can go in the direction you want to. The more your success in life will seem to 'just happen'. It doesn't just happen in some magical sense (I think), it happens because you are in ever better states of mind because you are en-joying your life.

People want to work with people who have a positive energy *and* who are good at what they do. How could it be any better? In looking after yourself, you help more people. When you help more people you make more money, and you can experience a lifestyle that supports your well-being... **and so the cycle spirals on upwards.**

I wish you many blessings along the way.

Please get in touch with any questions you may have. You can contact me through the website or via richard@richardingate.com

Notes:

Printed in Great Britain
by Amazon.co.uk, Ltd.,
Marston Gate.